Praise for "The #*%<!+& \

"Years from now, this book will be taught in histor
also funny as #>&%!" - Larry Doyle, Thurber Prize winning author

"If you want to understand what's gone on — what's gone wrong — during the Trump Years, there is no better guide than Ron Hauge. Always cheerful, weirdly sweet, this book is a sardonic, bug-eyed, candy-colored map of Hell, American Style." - Michael Gerber, Publisher; The American Bystander

"Ron Hauge combines a sophisticated comic mind with a broad burlesque style to create a series of unerring, mind-bendingly original political cartoons. And, in this writer's humble opinion, his drawings rank with the best American graphic art." - Stan Mack

"Ron Hauge's 'The #*%<!+& Year in Review' gives 2020 exactly what it deserves — a hilarious barrage of dark, acerbic humor (rendered in bright, comically cheerful colors!). The sensibility is irreverent, and funny as hell. If laughter really is the best medicine then Hauge is my new enterologist." - Barry Blitt

"Hauge's high-pitch electric-colored drawings land on their subjects like beautiful wrecking balls; heart-attacks of laughter, wit, spot-on observation and political activism in the hands of wicked-funny artist." - Jerry Saltz, Senior Art Critic; New York Magazine

"Ron Hauge's new book is a laugh-out-loud hilarious work of epic comic genius, a scathing dissection and a healing balm for the plague of the Trump presidency, culminating in its bumbling exacerbation of Covid. Hauge's unsparing pen pierces every festering nook and cranny of Trump's malicious incompetence, revealing them in dazzling, merciless epiphanies." - Mark Alan Stamaty

"Ron Hauge counters every outrage of this administration with drawings of wicked humor and righteous anger. He seems able to excavate ideas from any and every cultural reference and polish them into cartoons of devious absurdism, each one a destabilizing combination of wit and fury. Ron is a cartoonist of astonishing resourcefulness." - John Cuneo

"Thank you Ron for keeping me laughing throughout this Trump nightmare. Your daily fountain of cartoons has chronicled the whole sad story in surprising and delightful fashion. Seeing these villains skewered so skillfully has given me many moments of joy. Bravo!" - Mark Bryan

The #*%<!+& Year In Review

By Ron Hauge

HUMORIST
BOOKS

New York

First Edition: 2020

ISBN: 978-1-954158-02-3

Humorist Books is an imprint of *Weekly Humorist* owned and operated by Humorist Media LLC.

Weekly Humorist is a weekly humor publication, subscribe online at weeklyhumorist.com

110 Wall Street New York, NY 10005

weeklyhumorist.com - humoristbooks.com - humoristmedia.com

Table of Contents

1. The Life Pandemic

Broken Since March

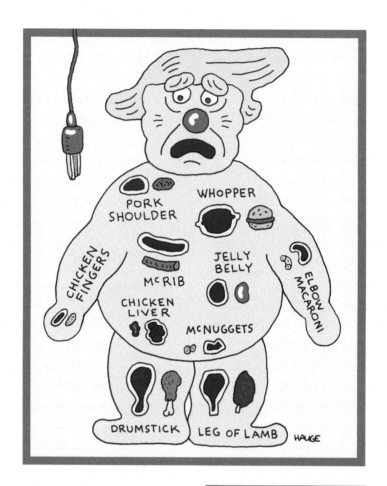

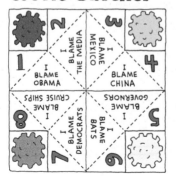

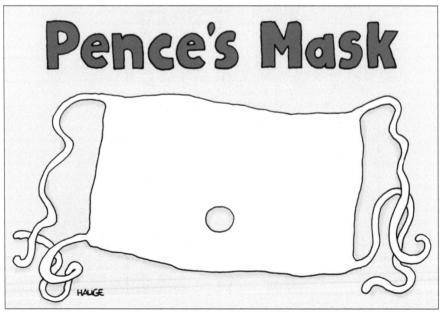

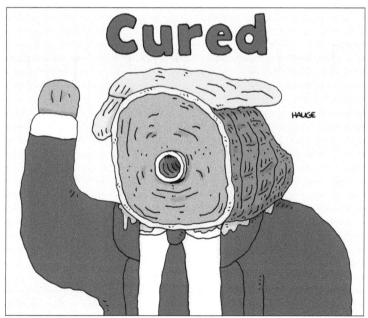

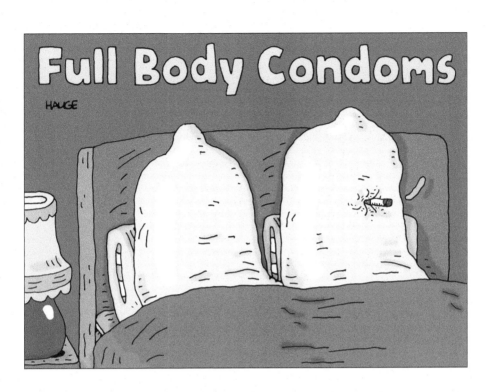

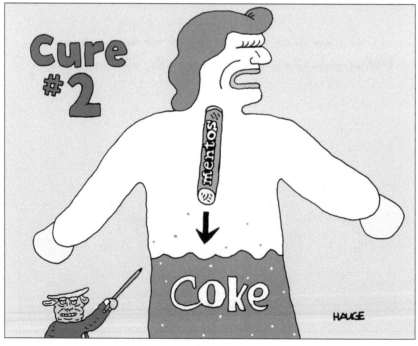

Thanksgiving 2020

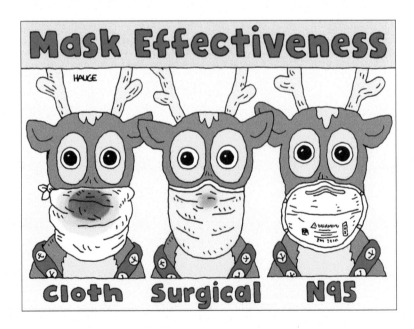

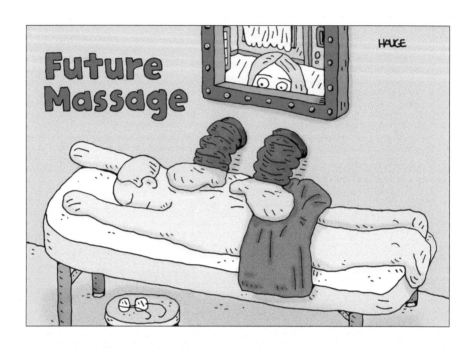

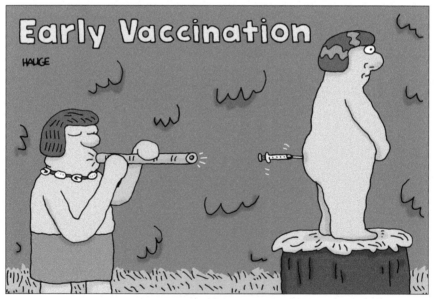

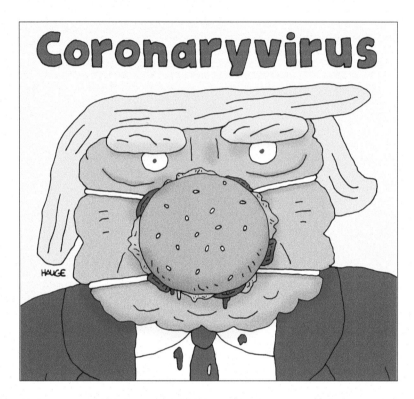

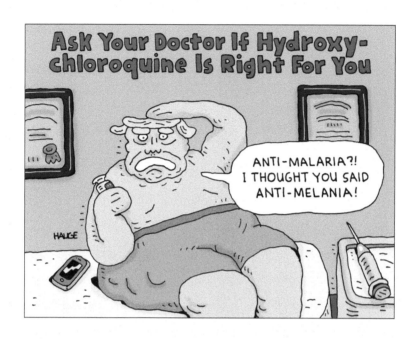

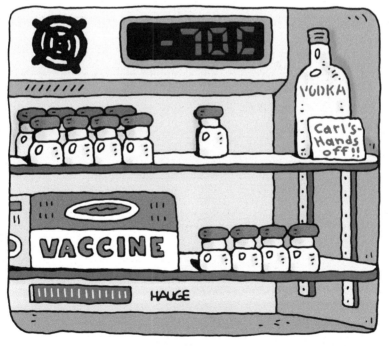

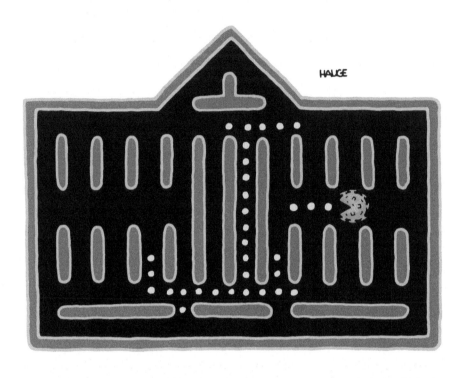

2. The Racist In Chief

Ku Klux Klown

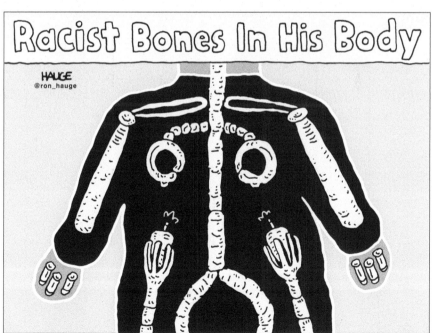

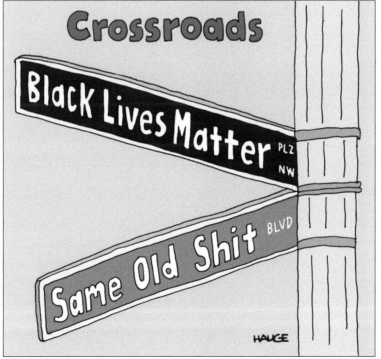

How Republican Parade Confetti Is Made

3. The Cray Cray

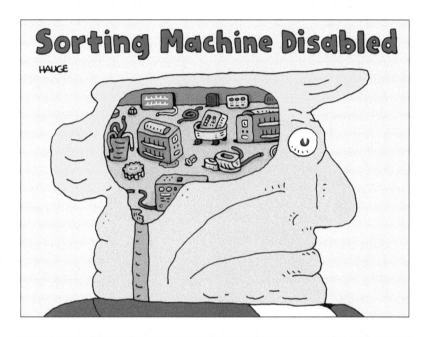

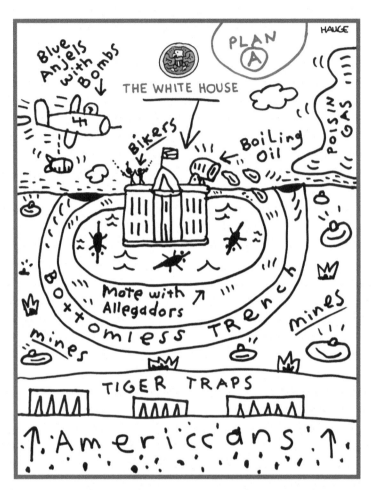

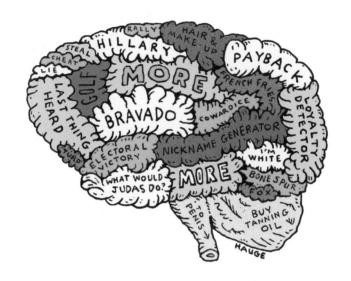

The Trump Presidential Library

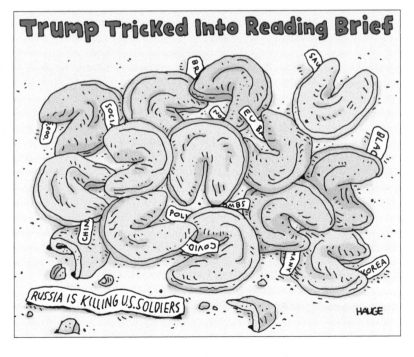

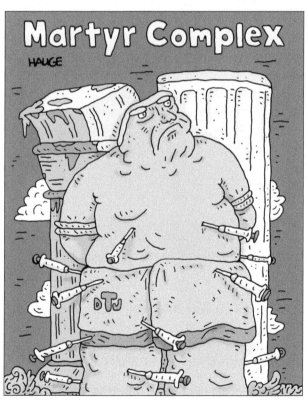

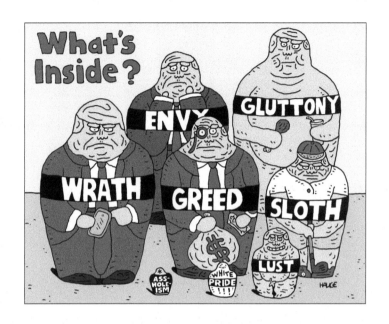

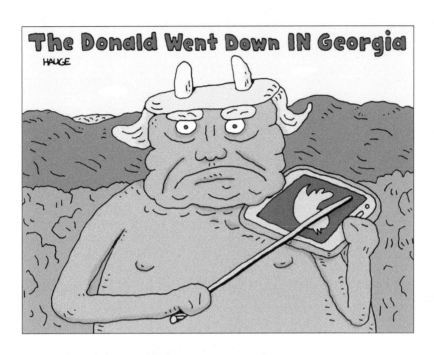

Boss Tweet

4. The Enablers

White House Staff Advised to Check Their Closets for Stephen Miller Before Bedtime

Mar-a-LEGO

Our Top Cop

... and this Little Piggy's house was built with Bill Barr and Mitch McConnell.

Constitution-proof Vest

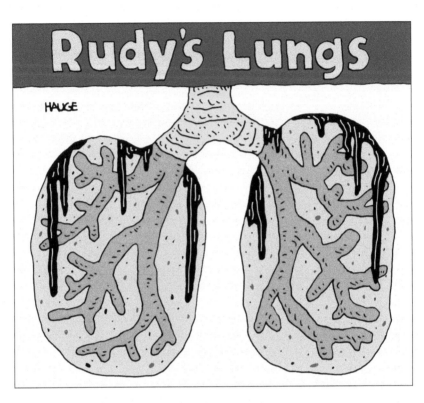

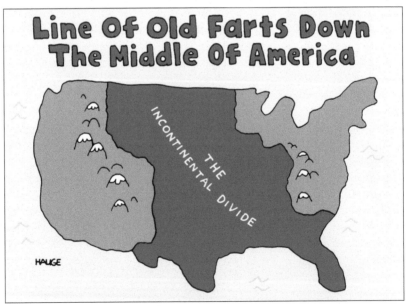

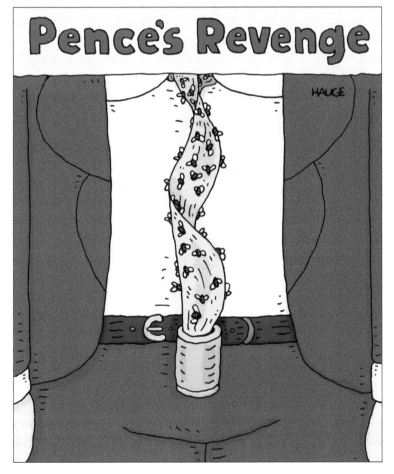

5. The Damage

How the Post Office Works

Improvised Election Device

Trump's Income

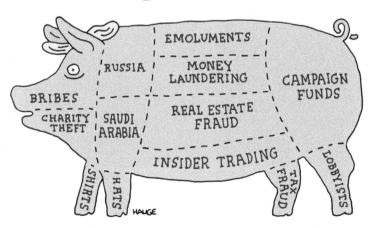

One Day It Will Just Disappear

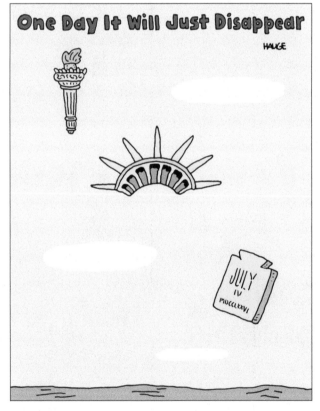

6. The Hope

Dried Up!

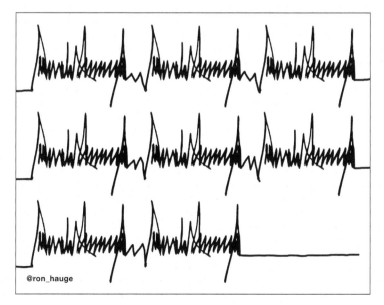

Ron Hauge

was a magazine artist and writer in New York before becoming
a full-time writer in California. His early drawings appeared in
"The National Lampoon," "The New York Times," "Time," "Harper's"
and many other publications. He has written for tv, film, print,
radio, video games and talking robots. Ron earned five Emmys as
a writer/producer at "The Simpsons," where he also supervised
the design work on the show for twelve years. He was previously
on the writing staffs of "Seinfeld," "In Living Color" and "The Ren &
Stimpy Show," and he was a guest writer on "Saturday Night Live."

Ron started drawing cartoons again about two and a half years
ago, to keep from personally exploding during the Trump years.
He hopes these cartoons will keep you from exploding, too.

Thanks!

Gary Baseman, Barry Blitt, Steve Brodner, Mark Bryan,
Jeff Christensen, John Cuneo, Larry Doyle, Marty Dundics,
Bob Eckstein, Renée Evans, Jessica Felleman, Michael
Gerber, Trevor Hoey, Al Jean, Chris Kelly, Jennifer Lyons,
Stan Mack, Bill Maher, Bob Mankoff, Andy Newton,
Jerry Saltz, Helene Silverman and Mark Alan Stamaty.